PROFILE OF THE WESTERNS

1029
D 1029

PROFILE OF THE WESTERNS

by
D. NICHOLAS
&
S. MONTGOMERY

Oxford Publishing Co.

Foreword

My first reaction to the news that 'Profile of the Westerns' was to be published was that of "What? Another book of Westerns!". Incredible though it may seem, even though no Class 52 has run in British Rail service for over three years, the enthusiasm for the class still seems to be very much in evidence. I first became acquainted with the class at their introduction for living as I then did at Plymouth I could witness the arrival of new members of the 'Hydraulic family' quite frequently.

Unlike many people in the early sixties whose sole interest was steam traction I devoted much of my spare time to observing and noting many changes which occurred in the diesel fleet. For example the modification and livery variations of the Class 52's alone could fill a small book. It was during my search for photographic material of the Class 52's that I first became acquainted with Dave Nicholas and Steve Montgomery, authors of this book and custodians of the Railway Museum at Dawlish Warren Station. There can be few people in a better position to write of the class for in those memorable days of 1975/6 when everyone it seemed was either falling into the sea to avoid the heat or falling into trains behind 'Westerns' to get haulage they were trying to run a museum with 'Westerns' literally roaring by only a few feet away.

The Class 52's are still to this day mourned by many. We all tend to suffer from nostalgia in one form or another to take our minds back to what we all enjoyed, and whether the class was in blue or earlier livery I am sure that this latest offering on the 'Westerns' will stir a few memories.

George G. Russum
Western Locomotive Association

Westbury-on-Trym
Bristol, July 1980

Plate 2 A regular working for 'Westerns', particularly during their later years, was the Cornish china clay traffic. D1023 *Western Fusilier* heads west from Dawlish with the Stoke-on-Trent to St. Blazey empties on 19th August, 1976.
L P Gater

Frontispiece:
Plate 1 Profile of a Western. D1029 *Western Legionnaire* poses for the camera outside Swindon Works in April 1969.
J G Glover

ISBN 0 86093 116 1

A FOULIS-OPC Railway Book

Published by:
Haynes Publishing Group
Sparkford, Near Yeovil, Somerset. BA22 7JJ

Haynes Publications Inc.
861 Lawrence Drive, Newbury Park, California 91320 USA

Introduction

When the 'Westerns' first took to the rails in 1961 they were despised by the railway enthusiast along with all the other diesel classes which had led to the ousting of their beloved steam. Yet only fourteen years later at their demise they attracted a following probably larger than that achieved by any other class of railway locomotive either before or since.

We lived with the three last summers of 'Western-mania' in the railway museum at Dawlish Warren and it is true to say that our lineside shop emptied quicker at the call of 'Wizzo' than it would have done at the call of 'Fire'. It was in these circumstances that we became addicted to these machines ourselves and it was with pleasure that we accepted the invitation to compile this album. Many photographs of the class have already been published but it is our intention that each photograph in this book should be new to print. This has not been produced as a work of reference as technical data has been published many times before and is now readily available. The contents have been selected to give pleasure and bring back happy memories.

Thanks to the efforts of the Western Locomotive Association D1062 *Western Courier* has been saved from extinction and together with its sister engine D1013 *Western Ranger*, privately owned but in their care, sees regular use. However, the cost of preservation does not end with the purchase price of a loco. It must not be forgotten that to enjoy the sight and distinctive sound of these machines in the future ongoing work and finance must be forthcoming to enable the Western Locomotive Association to maintain the machines in continuing preservation.

We would like to thank all those who have contributed to this volume and in particular Colin Marsden and George Russum for their valuable assistance.

D. Nicholas and S. Montgomery
Dawlish Warren Station, Devon. 1980.

Plate 3 A 'Western' at Crofton 1971. *Dawlish Warren Railway Museum*

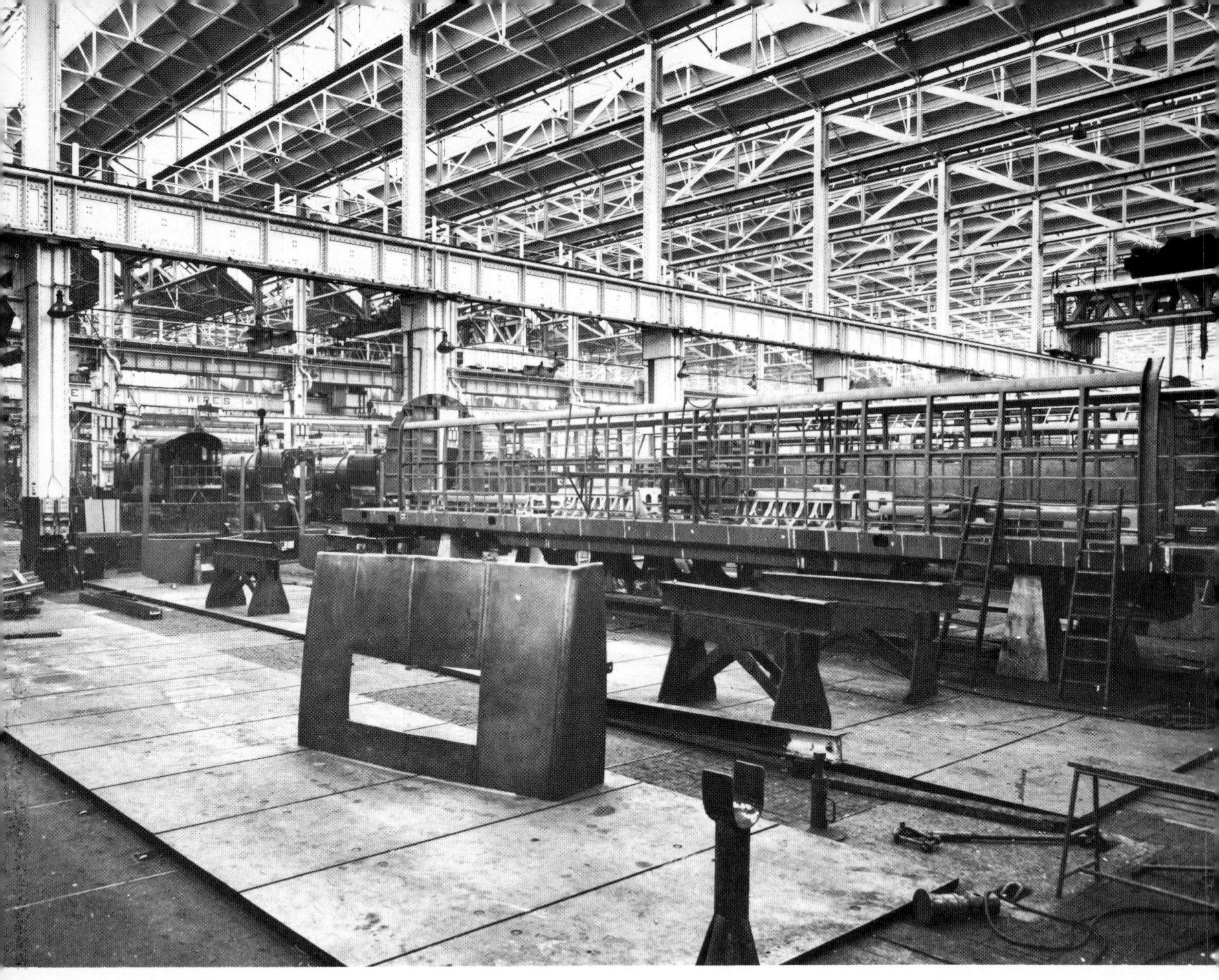

Plate 4 Construction of 'Westerns' in Swindon Works in 1961. The method of body shell fabrication can be clearly seen. Note the cab front in the foreground awaiting positioning.

C J Marsden Collection

BIRTH OF A CLASS

Plate 5 The finished product. The first of the class, D1000 *Western Enterprise*, stands outside Swindon Works prior to entering service in desert sand livery.

British Railways

Plate 6 One of the Crewe built members of the class recorded on trials while still in works primer. This photograph was taken on 29th March, 1963 but D1061 *Western Envoy* did not officially enter traffic until the 29th of the following month.

P J Chambers

Plate 7 A new and magnificent sight in the west! Less than two months into traffic D1000 *Western Enterprise* assists 'Warship' D866 *Zebra* with the 11.55 Manchester–Penzance train on its approach to Dainton Bank on 5th February, 1962.

C H S Owen

Plate 8 D1005 *Western Venturer* was numerically the second of the Swindon 'Westerns' to appear in the familiar maroon livery, but with an experimental buffer beam warning panel. This was later replaced by the standard half yellow end panel. It is here seen at Seer Green ten days into service on 28th June, 1962.

C J Marsden Collection

Plate 9 One of the three Swindon built members of the class to carry green livery, D1004 *Western Crusader* waits to leave Plymouth North Road for Paddington on 25th August, 1962.

Dawlish Warren Railway Museum

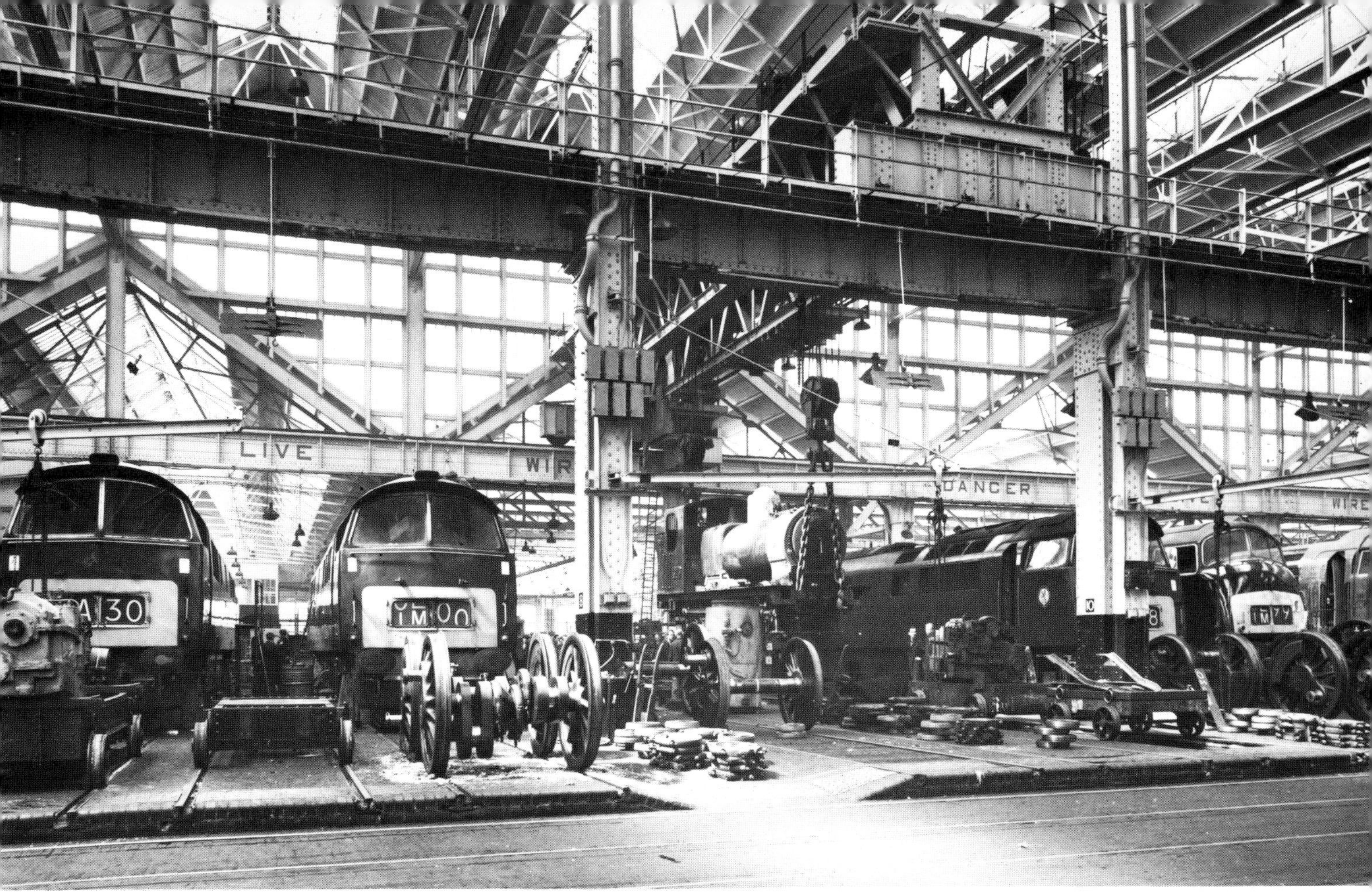

Plate 10 Transition at Swindon—Hydraulics dominate Swindon Works 'A' Shop but traces of steam still remain. The third 'Western' from the left is D1006 *Western Stalwart*.
C J Marsden Collection

Plate 11 A cab interior view of D1066 *Western Prefect*.

KEY

1. Straight air brake valve—locomotive only.
2. Air/vacuum brake valve—locomotive and train.
3. Main reservoir gauge.
4. Brake pipe gauge.
5. Bogie pressure gauge.
6. Vacuum train pipe/chamber gauge.
7. Speedometer.
8. RPM gauge.
9. Engine shed switch (on D1066 only).
10. A & B Engine start and stop buttons.
11. Tooth on tooth test button.
12. Window wiper air valves (2).
13. Fault lamps (5).
14. Air horn valve.
15. Rear cab horn button.
16. AWS reset button.
17. Forward—engine only—Reverse, master switch.
18. Power handle.

C J Marsden Collection

EXETER — Gateway to the West Country

Plate 12 What a journey! Diverted via the former Southern line between Plymouth and Exeter and then terminating at Kensington Olympia because of engineering work at Paddington. D1054 *Western Governor* enters Exeter from the east end with an eastbound train on 22nd October, 1967.

Dawlish Warren Railway Museum

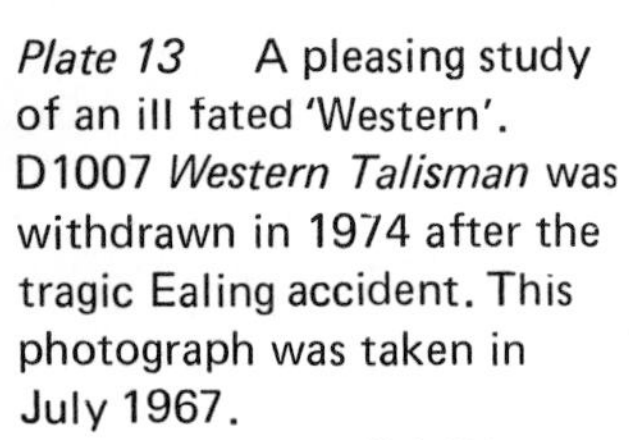

Plate 13 A pleasing study of an ill fated 'Western'. D1007 *Western Talisman* was withdrawn in 1974 after the tragic Ealing accident. This photograph was taken in July 1967.

Dawlish Warren Railway Museum

Plate 14 A less common position to photograph a train at Exeter. D1014 *Western Leviathan* waits to leave for Paddington with a through train from Barnstaple on 16th September, 1967. The 'Warship' which brought the train down from North Devon is still at the far end of the stock.

Dawlish Warren Railway Museum

Plate 15 Photographed from a train to Exeter Central D1001 *Western Pathfinder* with the well known 'Cornish Riviera Express' headcode stands waiting for the road on 21st August, 1972.
Dawlish Warren Railway Museum

Plate 16 One of the first 'Westerns' withdrawn, D1032 *Western Marksman* approaches St. David's station with an up motorail train on 27th July, 1969.
Dawlish Warren Railway Museum

CAPITAL APPROACH

Plate 17 A fine panoramic view of the approach to Paddington with D1065 *Western Consort* on an Inter-City arrival from Plymouth on 16th May, 1973.

Brian Morrison

Plate 18 A dated looking view of Paddington—even the diesel types have gone! On 8th October, 1964, D1061 *Western Envoy* waits near the 'Lawn' for a free road out of the station.
British Railways

Plate 19 Journey's end is near for D1049 *Western Monarch* as it passes under Ranelagh Bridge with an up train on 25th April, 1973.
Brian Morrison

Plate 20 Ranelagh Bridge must be familiar to all enthusiasts as the fuelling point for Paddington. On 15th January, 1969, D1025 *Western Guardsman* keeps company with another unfortunately unidentified 'Western'.

Dawlish Warren Railway Museum

Plate 21 Racing towards London through Sonning is D1030 *Western Musketeer* with its number in the headcode panel. As we type this caption we stand looking at the name and numberplates from this engine which are exhibits at Dawlish Warren Railway Museum.

John Vaughan

Plate 22 A clean maroon locomotive on blue and grey coaching stock. D1071 *Western Renown* was recorded at speed near Twyford in 1967.
C J Marsden Collection

Plate 23 D1061 *Western Envoy* on an up parcels train in Sonning Cutting, 20th July, 1974.
Geoff Dowling

Plate 24 Up through Somerset! D1033 *Western Trooper* approaches the site of Somerton station with the 06.35 Penzance–Paddington on 6th May, 1975.

John Cornelius

Plate 25 The 5A06, 06.50 Plymouth–Old Oak Common vans train passes Fairwood Junction, Westbury behind D1054 *Western Governor.*

Geoff Dowling

Plate 26 A busy spell at Totnes on 12th August, 1975. D1068 *Western Reliance* waits light engine in the platform road for D1056 *Western Sultan* to pass on a Paddington–Plymouth train. 'Peak' No. 46 004 is in the bay platform.

G W Morrison

Plate 27 D1059 *Western Empire* is held at the end of Exeter Riverside yard with ballast empties for Meldon Quarry while D1013 *Western Ranger* heads on towards Cowley Bridge Junction with a motorail train. 5th September, 1975.

L A Nixon

Plate 28 A maroon 'Western' on a matching rake of coaches shows to advantage the coach profile adopted in the design of the class. D1058 *Western Nobleman* has charge of a down South Wales express.

C J Marsden Collection

Plate 29 The down 'Riviera' curves through Castle Cary station behind D1016 *Western Gladiator* on 18th July, 1974.

Graham Scott-Lowe

Plate 30 Both the locomotive and the signals have disappeared from this scene near Hungerford. D1058 *Western Nobleman* snakes through the Berkshire countryside with a West of England train, the 13.30 Paddington—Penzance, on 14th August, 1976. ▷

Geoff Dowling

1058

WESTERN EMPIRE

Plate 32 Pulling away from Bristol Parkway station on 13th May, 1976 is D1072 *Western Glory* with the 13.15 Paddington—Cardiff.

Graham Scott-Lowe

Plate 31 An unusual view of D1059 *Western Empire* on the up through road at Totnes.

Geoff Dowling

Plate 33 Only six months away from withdrawal D1056 *Western Sultan* leaves Twerton Tunnel, Bath with the 09.30 Paddington—Paignton on 20th June, 1976.

Graham Scott-Lowe

Plate 34 Although latterly all members of the class were allocated to Laira they appeared regularly at most other depots on the region. D1041 *Western Prince* noses out of the fueller at Bristol Bath Road on 14th April, 1975.

Graham Scott-Lowe

ON SHED

Plate 35 Three hydraulic classes were represented at the Open Day at St. Blazey in May 1971. Specially cleaned for the occasion the 'Western' was D1056 *Western Sultan*. Clearly visible is the cab vent grill with its original louvre type cover.

Dawlish Warren Railway Museum

Plate 36 In their earlier years 'Westerns' were frequently to be found in and around steam sheds. D1028 *Western Hussar*, in maroon livery, was photographed at Swindon on 13th April, 1969. This engine was later fitted with a cab vent as seen in *Plate 135*.
John Cornelius

Plate 37 Only four weeks prior to withdrawal D1053 *Western Patriarch* still looks neat and presentable at Westbury on 16th October, 1976. Westbury was a favourite spot for 'Western' enthusiasts as the engines could be seen working stone trains to and from Merehead Quarry nearby.
G F Gillham

FREIGHT WORKINGS

Plate 38 Crossing back onto the down main line at Dawlish Warren after an unusual shunting movement in August 1972 is D1018 *Western Buccaneer*. This was one of the early withdrawals of the class, in June 1973, because it was not dual braked.

Dawlish Warren Railway Museum

Plate 39 The Acton–Norwood Junction coal train has 'Good power' on 24th March, 1976 as it passes through Kensington Olympia en route to the Southern Region behind D1021 *Western Cavalier.*

Brian Morrison

Plate 40 On the Plymouth Friary—Exeter Riverside freight in January 1977 is one of the last survivors of the class, D1048 *Western Lady*. This photograph was taken at Cockwood, between Starcross and Dawlish Warren.

Dawlish Warren Railway Museum

Plate 41 With the White Horse in the background D1021 *Western Cavalier* was recorded near Westbury on 11th May, 1976 with a block train of cement wagons.

Geoff Dowling

Plate 42 An unusual load! D1010 *Western Campaigner* is entrusted with LMS Pacific No. 6229 *Duchess of Hamilton* on its journey from Butlins Holiday Camp at Minehead to Swindon Works for restoration. The PW Gang at Castle Cary seem highly interested in the operation on 17th March, 1975.

Graham Scott-Lowe

Plate 43 Leaving the Drinnick Mill branch at Burngullow with a full load of china clay is D1039 *Western King* on 20th January, 1972.

Dawlish Warren Railway Museum

Plate 44 D1069 *Western Vanguard* pulls out of the now closed Exeter goods loop with a westbound train of oil tanks on 16th August, 1974.

John Cornelius

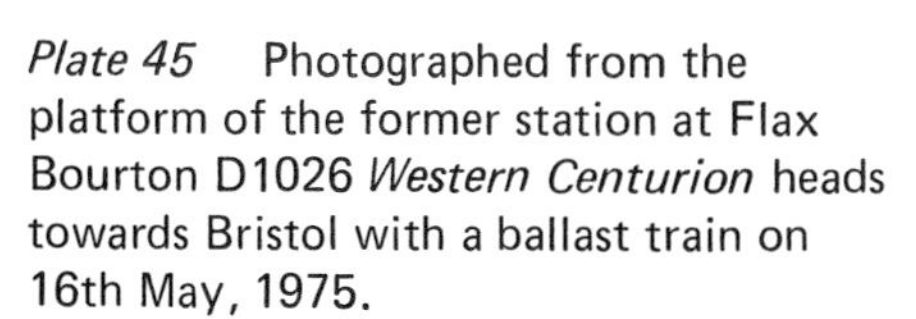

Plate 45 Photographed from the platform of the former station at Flax Bourton D1026 *Western Centurion* heads towards Bristol with a ballast train on 16th May, 1975.

Graham Scott-Lowe

TUNNELS

Plate 46 The classic shot. The western portal of Parson's Tunnel with D1037 *Western Empress* emerging into the sunshine with the 10.30 Paddington–Paignton train on 25th July, 1974.

N E Preedy

Plate 47 The 08.40 Penzance–Paddington train behind D1036 *Western Emperor* leaves Dainton Tunnel with an easy run down into Newton Abbot before it on 13th July, 1974.

G F Gillham

Plate 48 Under typical Brunel architecture D1034 *Western Dragoon* approaches Bath in 1968.

C J Marsden

Plate 49 Marking the boundary between Somerset and Devon is Whiteball Tunnel. Beginning its long descent towards Exeter is D1033 *Western Trooper.*

John Vaughan

Plate 50 Into Cornwall.
D1017 *Western Warrior* eases the 07.45 Kensington Olympia–St. Austell Motorail off the Royal Albert Bridge into Saltash station on 23rd August, 1972.
D H Allen

ACROSS THE TAMAR

Plate 51 Out of Cornwall.
Carrying the reporting number for the 11.00 Plymouth–Paddington train D1058 *Western Nobleman* enters Plymouth from Cornwall on 14th August, 1975.
G R Hounsell

Plate 52 Palm trees give a tropical atmosphere to Lostwithiel station as D1002 *Western Explorer* enters with a train for the Midlands on 17th July, 1971.
Dawlish Warren Railway Museum

Plate 53 A grey sunless Cornish sky overlooks D1071 *Western Renown* as it hurries along one of the few straight stretches of track in the county near Menheniot with the 08.00 train from Bristol to Penzance on 20th May, 1976.
John Vaughan

1053

Plate 55 D1033 *Western Trooper* climbs into St. Erth with an up train on 30th July, 1975.

Brian Morrison

Plate 56 A familiar view over the wall at Penzance. D1054 *Western Governor* backs onto the stock for the 16.10 train to Paddington on 23rd July, 1976.

John Vaughan

Plate 54 Curving away from Mounts Bay at the start of its journey north D1053 *Western Patriarch* passes the site of Marazion station with its Pullman camping coaches. The train is the 15.00 Penzance–Paddington on 7th July, 1976.

Brian Morrison

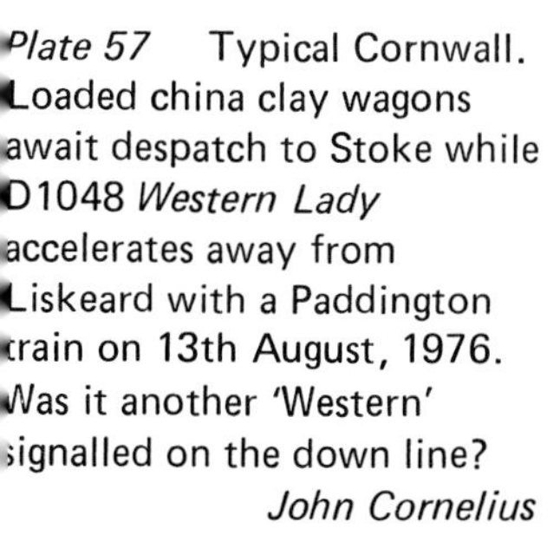

Plate 57 Typical Cornwall. Loaded china clay wagons await despatch to Stoke while D1048 *Western Lady* accelerates away from Liskeard with a Paddington train on 13th August, 1976. Was it another 'Western' signalled on the down line?

John Cornelius

50
1E22

9
CAR
1M19

◁ *Plate 58* With the Hayle Wharf line curving away on the left D1005 *Western Venturer* continues west on 26th July, 1975.

Brian Morrison

◁ *Plate 59* D1014 *Western Leviathan* with 14 on enters Lostwithiel with a train for the North on 17th July, 1971.

Dawlish Warren Railway Museum

Plate 60 D1022 *Western Sentinel* crosses one of the many Cornish Viaducts, near Chacewater.

Dawlish Warren Railway Museum

Plate 61 A summer haze hangs over Carn Brea as D1051 *Western Ambassador* heads the 08.00 Bristol–Penzance train on 5th July, 1976.

Brian Morrison

Plate 62 On 13th February, 1977 a relief was run a week before the main 'Western Requiem' railtour owing to the popularity of the event. D1010 *Western Campaigner* is ready to leave Cardiff Central for the return to Paddington after trips up three Welsh valley lines.
Graham Scott-Lowe

NIGHT PORTRAITS

Plate 63 Paddington station—the classic setting for this fine picture of D1015 *Western Champion* taken on 18th December, 1975.
R Watson

Plate 64 New Year's Day 1976 finds D1030 *Western Musketeer* in charge of the 15.30 Paddington–Penzance train as darkness begins to enshroud Reading station.

N E Preedy

Plate 65 The 03.13 down empty milk tanks to St. Erth pause at Plymouth behind D1065 *Western Consort* on 24th July, 1976.

John Vaughan

IN MAROON .

Plate 66 When maroon 'Westerns' first appeared they had yellow buffer beams as can be seen in this photograph of D1009 *Western Invader* only a month after it was taken into traffic. It is working the 09.30 train from Chester past Gresford Colliery Siding on 31st October, 1962.

OPC Collection

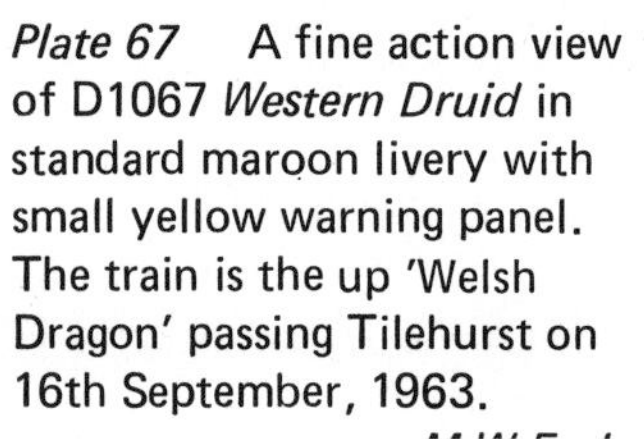

Plate 67 A fine action view of D1067 *Western Druid* in standard maroon livery with small yellow warning panel. The train is the up 'Welsh Dragon' passing Tilehurst on 16th September, 1963.

M W Earley

Plate 68 The later form of maroon livery, carried by twenty members of the class, was with a full yellow end. This is illustrated by D1045 *Western Viscount* leaving Exeter with a Manchester—Plymouth train.

Dawlish Warren Railway Museum

. . AND GREEN

Plate 69 In the quest for a new standard livery three Swindon-built and four Crewe-built engines were outshopped in Brunswick green with red buffer beams and small yellow warning panels. One of the Swindon representatives, D1003 *Western Pioneer*, is seen at Shaldon with the 11.30 Paddington–Penzance train on 7th July, 1962.

C H S Owen

Plate 70 One of the Crewe-built green locomotives, D1038 *Western Sovereign*, is seen here at Swindon in 1964. In this livery they carried red-backed name and numberplates which are clearly visible in this photograph. Three of the green members of the class, D1004/36/37 were the only ones never to carry maroon livery.

N E Preedy

ALONG THE COAST

Plate 71 The red cliffs of the South Devon coast echo to the sound of twin Maybach engines as D1051 *Western Ambassador* accelerates away from Teignmouth with the 10.00 Paignton–Paddington train on 14th June, 1975.
T G Flinders

Plate 72 On a hot and sultry day D1063 *Western Monitor* leans to the curve at Dawlish Warren with a train of rail in August 1972.
Dawlish Warren Railway Museum

Plate 73 With at least 12 on D1037 *Western Empress* roars past Langstone Cliff with 1A65, the 15.55 Paignton–Paddington working on 25th July, 1974.
N E Preedy

Plate 74 With the 10.30 Paddington–Penzance train D1035 *Western Yeoman* approaches the first of the five tunnels it will have to negotiate between Dawlish and Teignmouth. 30th April, 1972.
Dawlish Warren Railway Museum

Plate 75 Did any of these holiday-makers on 21st August, 1976 really appreciate the piece of history which was passing them? D1068 *Western Reliance* nears Teignmouth with the 08.30 Paddington–Paignton train.
Geoff Dowling

ON MILK

Plate 76 The first of the class, now in its third and final livery, heads the evening milk train north past Dawlish Warren.

Dawlish Warren Railway Museum

Plate 77 Once a regular duty at St. Erth D1013 *Western Ranger* shunts in the yard on 30th July, 1975 prior to departing with the milk train for Acton. Unfortunately this traffic has now ceased and the once commonplace six-wheeled tanks are greatly missed by those who watch the West of England main line.

Brian Morrison

Plate 78 A route not frequently travelled by 'Westerns' was the former Southern Railway line from Exeter to Plymouth. Diverted because of engineering work D1057 *Western Chieftain*, in chromatic blue livery, pauses at Lydford on 22nd October, 1967.

Dawlish Warren Railway Museum

Plate 79 Another former Southern line used for diversionary purposes is the Exeter–Yeovil Junction section of the line to Waterloo. At Talaton D1010 *Western Campaigner* was photographed on 14th April, 1974.

Dawlish Warren Railway Museum

Plate 80 Further east along the same line D1021 *Western Cavalier* is about to plunge into the darkness of Crewkerne Tunnel.

Dawlish Warren Railway Museum

IN EARLY BLUE LIVERY

Plate 81 Seven of the class were painted in a non-standard chromatic blue livery. The first of these, D1030 *Western Musketeer*, was the only one to be sprayed. It is here seen at Bristol Temple Meads on 21st June, 1969.

N E Preedy

Plate 82 In chromatic blue livery with small yellow warning panel D1043 *Western Duke* enters Exeter St. Davids station with a westbound train on 17th August, 1968.

Dawlish Warren Railway Museum

Plate 83 D1047 *Western Lord* enters Exeter from the west on 3rd August, 1968.
Dawlish Warren Railway Museum

Plate 84 A hazy day at the seaside. D1017 *Western Warrior* nears Dawlish with a down train.
Dawlish Warren Railway Museum

Plate 85 Newton Abbot on 4th April, 1969 and D1037 *Western Empress* waits for the 'right away'.
Dawlish Warren Railway Museum

Plate 86 A clear path from Taunton for D1071 *Western Renown* on the 11.55 Paignton—Paddington train on 21st April, 1976.
G F Gillham

UNDER SEMAPHORES

Plate 87 A fine gantry controls the western approach to Exeter St. Davids station. D1054 *Western Governor*, with a Gresley buffet vehicle at the front of its train, crosses the River Exe with the 09.45 Plymouth—Paddington on 13th July, 1976.
Brian Morrison

Plate 88   D1008 *Western Harrier* cautiously approaches Silk Mill Crossing at Taunton with a Plymouth–Manchester train on 19th November, 1971.

Dawlish Warren Railway Museum

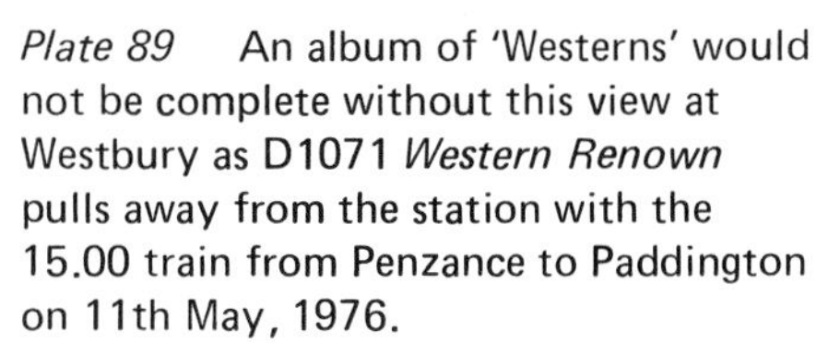

Plate 89   An album of 'Westerns' would not be complete without this view at Westbury as D1071 *Western Renown* pulls away from the station with the 15.00 train from Penzance to Paddington on 11th May, 1976.

Geoff Dowling

Plate 90 D1060 *Western Dominion* nears Cogload Junction with an engineers' train on 24th June, 1972.
John Cornelius

Plate 91 Far from its Western home D1022 *Western Sentinel* collects a rake of empty stone wagons at Luton on 21st September, 1976.
John Vaughan

Plate 92 An unusual duty for D1038 *Western Sovereign* is shunting the former Blue Anchor camping coaches at Taunton after their removal from the Minehead branch on 20th January, 1971.
John Cornelius

IRREGULAR DUTIES

Plate 93 On what is normally Class 37 territory D1045 *Western Viscount* trundles through Ebbw Vale steel works with a van train.

Graham Scott-Lowe

Plate 94 A trail of delays. An already diverted Swansea–Paddington working comprising air-conditioned stock has been held for fitters to attend to D1005 *Western Venturer* at Westbury on 2nd May, 1976.

Graham Scott-Lowe

CAMERA SHY MACHINES

Plate 95 Certain members of the class seemed to evade the photographers more than others. A study of one of the earlier withdrawals, D1024 *Western Huntsman*, at Exeter in August 1967.

Dawlish Warren Railway Museum

Plate 96 D1011 *Western Thunderer* on the Devon side of the Royal Albert Bridge with an inter-regional train in June 1974.

N E Preedy

Plate 97 D1060 *Western Dominion* pauses at Dawlish with a westbound train on 11th August, 1968.

Dawlish Warren Railway Museum

Plate 98 The standard platform 1 study at Exeter St. Davids of D1031 *Western Rifleman* on 21st August, 1972.

Dawlish Warren Railway Museum

Plate 99 Perhaps the least photographed of all? Allocated for just over half of its working life in South Wales D1066 *Western Prefect* was recorded at Horton Road depot, Gloucester on 16th September, 1970.

N E Preedy

Plate 100 Creating a lot of interest after having emerged from Swindon Works D1042 *Western Princess* was filmed from a passing train on 25th September, 1970.

Dawlish Warren Railway Museum

Plate 101 In comparison with D1056 in *Plate 35* D1020 *Western Hero* was a far less respectable exhibit for the St. Blazey Open Day in 1971.

Dawlish Warren Railway Museum

RAILS TO THE WEST

Plate 102 D1009 *Western Invader* passes through Slough with the 12.30 Paddington—Penzance on 3rd October, 1976. It has been diverted on to the slow lines because of engineering work.

John Vaughan

Plate 103 One of the class which was never air-braked and was therefore an early victim of withdrawal was D1019 *Western Challenger* captured by the camera on a down train at Theale on 24th July, 1971.

Dawlish Warren Railway Museum

Plate 104 D1044 *Western Duchess* arrives at Reading with an evening train from Paddington to Weston-super-Mare on 9th April, 1974.

B J Nicolle

Plate 105 Another view of a westbound train at Reading, this time the 11.30 Paddington–Penzance, behind D1050 *Western Ruler* on 16th April, 1974.

N E Preedy

Plate 106 A favourite photographic location. D1046 *Western Marquis* is neatly framed between two signals as it speeds west through Sonning Cutting on 3rd August, 1974.

Geoff Dowling

Plate 108 D1070 *Western Gauntlet* hurries along the Westbury avoiding line towards Fairwood Junction with the 13.30 train from Paddington to Penzance.

N E Preedy

Plate 107 A bright morning in early spring finds D1064 *Western Regent* passing the stark war-time signal box at Castle Cary with the 09.30 Paddington–Penzance in March 1975.

Graham Scott-Lowe

Plate 109 D1057 *Western Chieftain* pounds through the Somerset countryside near Witham with the 12.30 train to Paignton on 26th August, 1974.

G F Gillham

Plate 110 After crossing the London line D1041 *Western Prince* drops down from the flyover for the run into Taunton with the 10.24 Manchester–Plymouth train on 5th April, 1974.

G F Gillham

Plate 111 D1067 *Western Druid* slows down as it approaches Castle Cary with the 10.05 train from Weymouth to Bristol on 17th March, 1975. It will join the West of England main line as far as Westbury and then take the line to Bristol through Trowbridge and Bath.

Graham Scott-Lowe

Plate 112 D1036 *Western Emperor*, easily recognisable by its higher level numberplate, passes the site of Patney and Chirton station where the original line through Devizes diverged from the present main line. The train is the 06.35 Penzance–Paddington on 31st March, 1975.

G F Gillham

Plate 113 In maroon livery with yellow buffer beam D1006 *Western Stalwart* enters Taunton with a train for the west on 11th August, 1962. Note the up bay starter signal on the left.

John Cornelius

Plate 114 With load 13 on, D1027 *Western Lancer* approaches Taunton station with a London train on 14th September, 1968.

John Cornelius

Plate 115 The 12.30 Paddington–Paignton train descends from Whiteball Tunnel on a 1 in 115 falling gradient behind D1017 *Western Warrior* on 20th May, 1972.

Dawlish Warren Railway Museum

Plate 116 A fine study of the last of the class D1073 *Western Bulwark* as it draws away from Exeter on 28th June, 1969.
Dawlish Warren Railway Museum

Plate 117 Speeding through the Warren. D1069 *Western Vanguard* heads west towards the seawall at Dawlish Warren on 23rd August, 1972.
Dawlish Warren Railway Museum

Plate 118 On a summer Saturday only train, the 12.05 from Newquay—Nottingham, D1052 *Western Viceroy* rounds the curve at Aller Junction on 9th August, 1975.
L P Gater

OVER THE BANKS

Plate 119 Back to Laira. A pair of 'Thousands', D1049 *Western Monarch* and D1048 *Western Lady*, running light on a 1 in 52 gradient near Tigley on 9th September, 1975.

Geoff Dowling

Plate 120 D1021 *Western Cavalier* drops down into Totnes from Rattery with the 09.50 Plymouth–Paddington on 6th September, 1975.

Geoff Dowling

Plate 121 Totnes station and D1062 *Western Courier*, in weatherbeaten maroon livery, enters the down platform loop with a freight train in October 1966.
Dawlish Warren Railway Museum

Plate 122 The westbound 'Cornish Riviera Express' passes the site of Brent station, formerly the junction for the Kingsbridge Branch, behind D1027 *Western Lancer*, on 6th September, 1975.
Geoff Dowling

WESTERNS WELSH

Plate 126 D1023 *Western Fusilier* ▷ heading the 'Western Requiem' rail tour of the Welsh Valleys, forges up the Merthyr Tydfil Branch near Merthyr Vale on 20th February, 1977.

L A Nixon

Plate 127 With its red-backed name and numberplate D1013 *Western Ranger* heads the 08.55 Swansea—Paddington train away from Newport on 12th August, 1976.

Geoff Dowling ▷

Plate 123 Set against the familiar backcloth of Cardiff Central station D1011 *Western Thunderer* enters with the 13.15 train to Paddington on 5th June, 1973.

N E Preedy

Plate 124 The east end of Cardiff General station complete with its Great Western searchlight colour light signals is the setting for D1059 *Western Empire* on a westbound freight in 1964.

Dawlish Warren Railway Museum

Plate 125 D1021 *Western Cavalier* hurries a down South Wales express away from Cardiff towards Rumney River Bridge signal box on 19th May, 1964.

S Rickard

WESTERN
REQUIEM
18-6 5
20
E10
1013

AROUND BRISTOL

Plate 128 As yet without cab vent D1012 *Western Firebrand*, in maroon livery with full yellow end, waits to leave Bristol Temple Meads with a Paddington train on 19th October, 1968.

Dawlish Warren Railway Museum

Plate 129 Watched by youthful admirers D1057 *Western Chieftain* awaits the right away with the 11.15 Bristol–Cardiff on 20th February, 1975.

Graham Scott-Lowe

Plate 130 A popular engine, D1041 *Western Prince* stands ready to take over from a 'Peak' on a train from the north on 30th April, 1966.
Dawlish Warren Railway Museum

Plate 131 The 12.15 Bristol–Paddington train forges through Keynsham station behind D1071 *Western Renown* on 19th June, 1974.
Graham Scott-Lowe

Plate 132 A Sunday afternoon Paddington–Bristol–Paignton train pauses in the twilight at Temple Meads with D1022 *Western Sentinel* on 14th November, 1976.
▽ *Dawlish Warren Railway Museum*

Plate 133 D1072 *Western Glory* speeds west between Nailsea & Backwell and Yatton on 15th November, 1970.
Dawlish Warren Railway Museum ▷

'THE BRANCH'

Plate 134 A line not often photographed is what is known locally as 'The Branch'—from Newton Abbot to Paignton and Kingswear. D1002 *Western Explorer* accelerates away from Aller Junction in high summer on 18th August, 1972.

Dawlish Warren Railway Museum

Plate 135 An up train leaves Paignton on 6th August, 1975 behind D1028 *Western Hussar*.

Brian Morrison

Plate 136 Both the footbridge and level crossing gates at the north end of Paignton station have now been replaced. On 1st May, 1969 D1065 *Western Consort* draws into the station with a short local train.

Dawlish Warren Railway Museum

Plate 137 The crossing gates at Sands Road, the south end of Paignton station, are fortunately still intact. D1015 *Western Champion* takes the stock into the station from Goodrington carriage sidings for the 17.55 train to Bristol on 6th August, 1975.

Brian Morrison

Plate 138 A study of D1002 *Western Explorer* in the down platform at Paignton on 3rd November, 1969.
Dawlish Warren Railway Museum

Plate 141 A cab view of D1036 *Western Emperor* at Reading. Note the driver's ticket clip below the side window which was only on Crewe-built members of the class. As mentioned previously, the numberplate on this engine was mounted higher on the cabside than all the others to enable the fitting of experimental AWS apparatus in the cab. ▷
Geoff Dowling

Plate 139 The beautiful wooded valley at the side of the Dart echoes to the sound of D1045 *Western Viscount* as it climbs towards Churston from Greenway Tunnel with a Kingswear–Paddington train on 28th August, 1971. This engine is recognisable by the windscreen wiper on the secondman's side which is mounted below, rather than above, the window.
Dawlish Warren Railway Museum

Plate 140 D1009 *Western Invader* waiting for the road away from Paignton on 10th August, 1976.
John Cornelius

D 1036
1C36

Plate 142 The 'Cambrian Coast Express' passes Stow Heath Siding, Wolverhampton, with D1034 *Western Dragoon* at the head in immaculate maroon livery on 25th February, 1965. Note the mixture of upper and lower quadrant signalling.
OPC Collection

Plate 143 Under the wires at Birmingham New Street on a wet June day in 1976. The engine is D1072 *Western Glory*, no doubt about to return west. On the driver's front window are the remains of the fittings for a lateral windscreen wiper which this engine once carried.
John Cornelius

THE MIDLANDS

Plate 144 D1037 *Western Empress* passes through Widney Manor between Birmingham and Leamington Spa with the 10.25 Paddington train ex Birmingham on 5th July, 1975.

Geoff Dowling

SWINDON WORKS

Plate 145 D1023 *Western Fusilier* receives one of its quota of two Maybach MD655 engines during its last general overhaul.

British Railways

Plate 146 The body of *Western Fusilier* is lowered onto its bogies in the erecting shop in February 1973. This engine was the last member of the class to receive a general overhaul and after withdrawal in February 1977 was preserved as part of the National Railway Museum collection.

British Railways

Plate 147 D1032 *Western Marksman* receives the Swindon Works treatment on 13th April, 1969. This locomotive was one of the first withdrawn (on 6th May, 1973), having been out of traffic since 16th January, 1973 because no engines were available for it.

John Cornelius

Plate 148 Ready for service. D1047 *Western Lord* in maroon livery on 8th September, 1963.

John Cornelius

Plate 149 In their latter days in particular the 'Westerns' appeared frequently on stone workings. On 14th July, 1976 D1072 *Western Glory* is framed by the conveyor at Tytherington Quarry on the reopened section of the former Midland Railway branch to Thornbury.

Graham Scott-Lowe

Plate 150 With a block train of 'Yeoman' hoppers D1015 *Western Champion* leaves the main line at Fairwood Junction for the yard at Westbury on 9th July, 1975. This train has come from Merehead Quarry on the former Cheddar Valley branch line from Witham.

Graham Scott-Lowe

STONE

Plate 151 D1048 *Western Lady* waits alongside Bristol Parkway station with a stone train from Tytherington on 13th May, 1976.

Graham Scott-Lowe

Plate 152 An obviously keen gardener tends his allotment as D1040 *Western Queen* works past with the Botley–Westbury stone empties on 9th April, 1974. The location is Salisbury, with the cathedral spire hardly visible in the background mist.

G F Gillham

Plate 153 Ballast empties for Stoneycombe Quarry near Newton Abbot skirt the Teign Estuary opposite Shaldon behind D1055 *Western Advocate* on 23rd August, 1972.

Dawlish Warren Railway Museum

Plate 154 D1023 *Western Fusilier* descends from Treverrin Tunnel near Par with a ballast train on 21st May, 1976.

John Vaughan

ON TOUR

Plate 155 Towards the end of their working life the 52's were in great demand for railtours and were to be found in unlikely areas. D1010 *Western Campaigner* leaves Newport with the 'Western Requiem' railtour from Paddington to the Welsh Valleys on 20th February, 1977 a week before its final withdrawal.

L A Nixon

Plate 156 A momentous occasion was the WLA 'Western Talisman' run from King's Cross to York on 20th November, 1976. D1023 *Western Fusilier* is seen climbing Holloway Bank on the East Coast Main Line in North London. This engine was the only 'Western' to carry the white marker dots in service as they were a requirement for working this rail-tour on the Eastern Region.

Brian Morrison

Plate 157 D1023 *Western Fusilier* found its way to York, now its new home, once again on 12th February, 1977 with an Exeter–York excursion. This photograph shows it negotiating Marsh Lane Cutting at Leeds. The locomotive shows damage on the front skirting caused when it hit a cow at Charfield earlier in the day.

L A Nixon

Plate 158 The last 'Western' hauled normal service train out of Paddington was the 10.40 to Plymouth on 8th February, 1977. D1023 *Western Fusilier* is seen at Westbury on this train.
Colin Marsden

Plate 159 The very last 'Western' hauled train in BR service was their own 'Western Tribute' railtour on 26th February, 1977 from Paddington–Swansea–Plymouth–Paddington. The train is seen leaving Paddington with D1023 *Western Fusilier* and D1013 *Western Ranger* in charge.
Brian Morrison

FINAL WORKINGS

Plate 160 After withdrawal in January 1975 D1003 *Western Pioneer* languished in Swindon yard awaiting the cutter's torch and was photographed there in March 1977 after all the remaining members of the class had also been withdrawn.
Colin Marsden

DEATH . . .

Plate 161 D1043 *Western Duke* undergoes the ultimate fate for all but the lucky few 'Thousands'. The transmission goes under the torch on 31st January, 1977.
Graham Scott-Lowe

. . . REBIRTH AND REFLECTION

Plate 162 Thanks to the efforts of the Western Locomotive Association and its members D1062 *Western Courier* has been saved and is seen here climbing Highley Bank on the Severn Valley Railway in October 1979.

Jeremy De Souza

Plate 163 Reflection at Swindon in 1977.

John Vaughan

'WESTERN' Class 52 Locomotive Summary

No.	Name	Date to Traffic	Last day in Traffic	Date Withdrawn	Mileage
D1000	Western Enterprise	20.12.61	7.2.74	11.2.74	1,200,000
D1001	Western Pathfinder	12.2.62	3.10.76	4.10.76	1,264,000
D1002	Western Explorer	19.3.62	26.1.74	29.1.74	1,144,000
D1003	Western Pioneer	14.4.62	16.9.74	6.1.75	1,248,000
D1004	Western Crusader	12.5.62	24.7.73	1.8.73	1,088,000
D1005	Western Venturer	18.6.62	13.11.76	14.11.76	1,392,000
D1006	Western Stalwart	6.6.62	31.3.75	4.4.75	1,208,000
D1007	Western Talisman	1.8.62	19.12.73	29.1.74	1,160,000
D1008	Western Harrier	4.9.62	24.8.74	21.10.74	1,136,000
D1009	Western Invader	24.9.62	9.11.76	10.11.76	1,376,000
D1010	Western Campaigner	15.10.62	27.2.77	27.2.77	1,360,000
D1011	Western Thunderer	27.10.62	2.10.75	6.10.75	1,248,000
D1012	Western Firebrand	17.11.62	1.11.75	1.11.75	1,296,000
D1013	Western Ranger	3.12.62	27.2.77	27.2.77	1,320,000
D1014	Western Leviathan	24.12.62	9.6.74	8.8.74	1,128,000
D1015	Western Champion	21.1.63	8.12.76	13.12.76	1,296,000
D1016	Western Gladiator	16.2.63	28.12.75	30.12.75	1,248,000
D1017	Western Warrior	15.3.63	19.7.73	1.8.73	984,000
D1018	Western Buccaneer	2.4.63	1.6.73	4.6.73	968,000
D1019	Western Challenger	2.5.63	1.5.73	6.5.73	968,000
D1020	Western Hero	21.5.63	18.5.73	4.6.73	968,000
D1021	Western Cavalier	17.6.63	9.8.76	10.8.76	1,280,000
D1022	Western Sentinel	16.7.63	18.1.77	26.1.77	1,312,000
D1023	Western Fusilier	23.9.63	27.2.77	27.2.77	1,256,000
D1024	Western Huntsman	1.10.63	5.10.73	17.11.73	984,000
D1025	Western Guardsman	1.11.63	5.10.75	6.10.75	1,192,000
D1026	Western Centurion	24.12.63	5.10.75	6.10.75	1,144,000
D1027	Western Lancer	29.1.64	1.11.75	1.11.75	1,176,000
D1028	Western Hussar	29.2.64	5.10.76	5.10.76	1,256,000
D1029	Western Legionnaire*	14.7.64	18.11.74	18.11.74	1,056,000
D1030	Western Musketeer	5.12.63	18.4.76	19.4.76	1,216,000
D1031	Western Rifleman	20.12.63	2.12.74	3.2.75	1,096,000
D1032	Western Marksman	31.12.63	16.1.73	6.5.73	994,000
D1033	Western Trooper	17.1.64	15.9.76	16.9.76	1,272,000
D1034	Western Dragoon	15.4.64	7.10.75	9.10.75	1,144,000
D1035	Western Yeoman	27.7.62	28.12.74	6.1.75	1,176,000
D1036	Western Emperor	29.8.62	29.10.76	29.10.76	1,360,000
D1037	Western Empress	31.8.62	19.5.76	23.5.76	1,336,000
D1038	Western Sovereign	9.9.62	15.8.73	8.10.73	1,072,000
D1039	Western King	7.9.62	1.3.74	21.7.74	1,024,000
D1040	Western Queen	20.9.62	26.2.76	29.2.76	1,248,000
D1041	Western Prince	10.10.62	22.2.77	22.2.77	1,384,000
D1042	Western Princess	19.10.62	18.4.74	21.7.74	976,000
D1043	Western Duke	26.10.62	4.4.76	5.4.76	1,304,000
D1044	Western Duchess	12.11.62	31.1.75	2.2.75	1,208,000
D1045	Western Viscount	16.11.62	3.12.74	17.12.74	1,192,000
D1046	Western Marquis	24.12.62	5.12.75	7.12.75	1,248,000
D1047	Western Lord	4.12.63	1.3.76	7.3.76	1,256,000
D1048	Western Lady	15.12.62	27.2.77	27.2.77	1,368,000
D1049	Western Monarch	24.12.62	22.4.76	22.4.76	1,288,000
D1050	Western Ruler	1.1.63	28.3.75	4.4.75	1,176,000
D1051	Western Ambassador	21.1.63	1.9.76	2.9.76	1,328,000
D1052	Western Viceroy	4.2.63	28.8.75	6.10.75	1,224,000
D1053	Western Patriarch	11.2.63	13.11.76	13.11.76	1,304,000
D1054	Western Governor	2.3.63	24.11.76	25.11.76	1,336,000
D1055	Western Advocate	2.3.63	3.1.76	5.1.76	1,200,000
D1056	Western Sultan	8.3.63	15.12.76	15.12.76	1,352,000
D1057	Western Chieftain	6.4.63	1.5.76	2.5.76	1,296,000
D1058	Western Nobleman	25.3.63	20.1.77	21.1.77	1,312,000
D1059	Western Empire	6.4.63	6.10.75	6.10.75	1,216,000
D1060	Western Dominion	11.4.63	17.7.73	17.11.73	1,032,000
D1061	Western Envoy	19.4.63	4.8.74	21.10.74	1,104,000
D1062	Western Courier	6.5.63	26.7.74	23.8.74	1,096,000
D1063	Western Monitor	17.5.63	3.4.76	4.4.76	1,184,000
D1064	Western Regent	24.5.63	5.12.75	7.12.75	1,216,000
D1065	Western Consort	18.6.63	30.10.76	30.10.76	1,288,000
D1066	Western Prefect	14.6.63	11.11.74	11.11.74	1,032,000
D1067	Western Druid	18.7.63	14.1.76	15.1.76	1,232,000
D1068	Western Reliance	12.7.63	11.10.76	13.10.76	1,312,000
D1069	Western Vanguard	21.10.63	4.10.75	6.10.75	1,168,000
D1070	Western Gauntlet	28.10.63	30.12.76	30.12.76	1,312,000
D1071	Western Renown	7.11.63	7.12.76	8.12.76	1,232,000
D1072	Western Glory	7.11.63	2.11.76	2.11.76	1,280,000
D1073	Western Bulwark	3.12.63	28.8.74	29.8.74	1,048,000

Aggregate mileage of fleet: 88,060,000 miles

Average miles per locomotive: 1,190,000 miles

* D1029 ran as Western Legionaire until 1967

Livery summary *(courtesy WLA)*

Desert Sand	D1000
Golden Ochre	D1015
Maroon/Yellow buffer beam	D1001/5/6/7/8/9/39/40/41/42
Green/half yellow panel	D1002/3/4/35/36/37/38
Maroon/half yellow panel	All except D1004/36/37
Maroon/full yellow end	D1001/2/7/8/12/16/25/31/32/39/41/44/45/46/54/56/61/67/68
Blue/half yellow panel	D1017/36/37/43/47/57
Blue/half yellow/red buffer beam	D1030
Blue/Full yellow end	ALL